3-10

Jig Jiggle Sneeze

Written by **Joy Vitalis**

Illustrated by **Jan Dolby**

Magic W★rld
m e d i a

Rhina O'Virus quivered with excitem[ent.]
She had floated and
swirled . . .
and drifted an[d]
sailed . . .
and now,
finally, she fou[nd]
herself in
a nice warm place.

2

She set off to explore.

Through the tall, tall forest, up and down, around one tree, then another . . . . . . and there they were, rows and rows of buildings, stretching as far as she could see.

4

"Perfect," Rhina snickered, "I'm moving in!"

But how would she get in? The doors were all locked tight and there were sure to be policemen who might recognize and capture her.

"Hah!" smirked Rhina. "I'm not scared. I have a secret. I have a special key."

Rhina looked up.
There were thousands
of buildings. And each building
had hundreds of doors,
    all different shapes and sizes.
Surely her key would open one of them.

            She floated up and down and
                around and around,

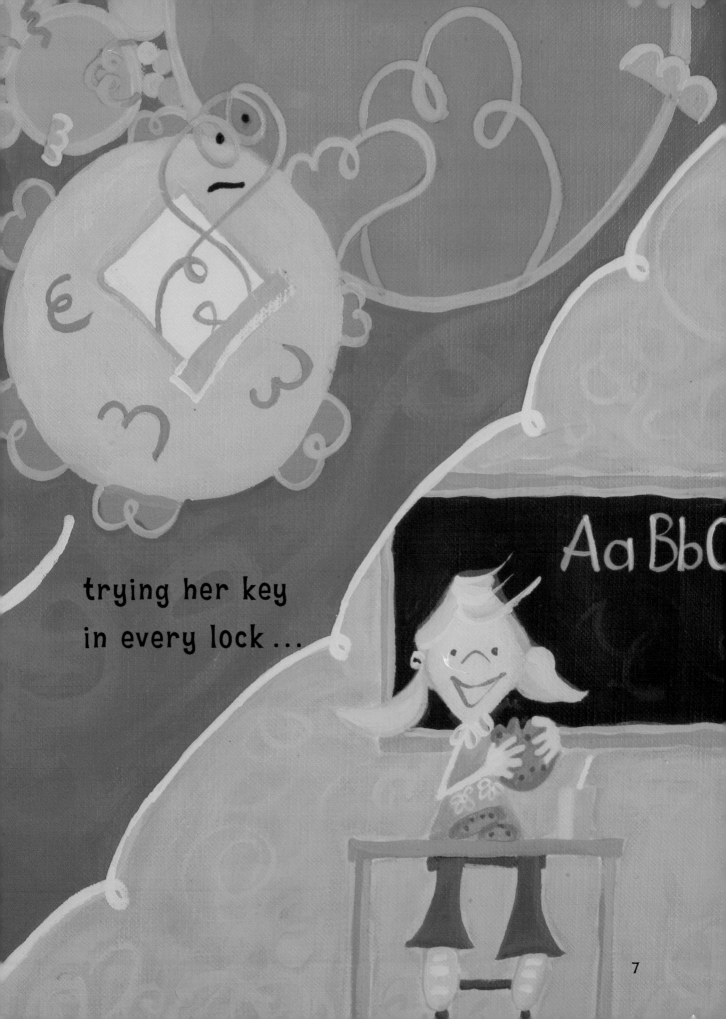

trying her key
in every lock ...

7

. . . until CLICK!

A door swung open
and let her in.

Rhina wriggled out of her space suit.

She jumped
and slid
and banged around.

She kicked things and hung
upside down. She poked
around and . . .

8

. . . look what
she found!
"**Copying machines!**" Rhina squealed.
"I'll copy myself!" she said with glee.

"Then I'll have friends to play with and a big, **BIG party.**"
And she began to make copies of herself.
Rhinnifer and Rhinata, Rhin-Rhin and Rhinee, Rhinea and Rhinsey
. . . And soon, she had made almost four thousand,
two hundred and seventeen O'Viruses just

like herself.

The place
was bursting.
There was
hardly room
for them all!

They jigged and they jiggled.
They wiggled and danced.
They rollicked and frolicked.
They played hide and seek.

They played Marco Polo.
And they made a big, big mess.

And still Rhina made more O'Viruses and the
mess grew, and
grew, and
grew
until...

POLO

12

it was simply
too crowded.

Rhina gathered them all. "There is no room here," she told them. "Go find new places to stay and make new friends to play with."

And they did. And soon, there were one hundred million, eight thousand, two hundred and forty-four of them.

All making a MESS!

Until . . .

Uh-oh. What was that?

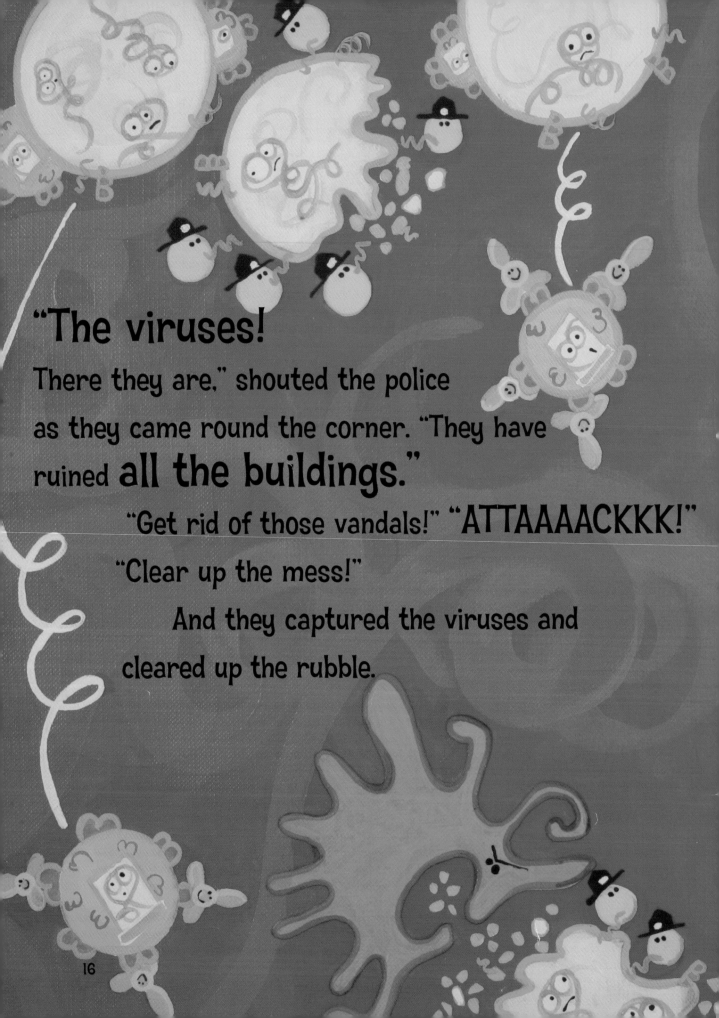

"The viruses!
There they are," shouted the police
as they came round the corner. "They have
ruined **all the buildings.**"

"Get rid of those vandals!" "ATTAAAACKKK!"

"Clear up the mess!"

And they captured the viruses and
cleared up the rubble.

Then suddenly . . .
Whoosh!
What was that?
That whoosh,
whistle,
rumble?

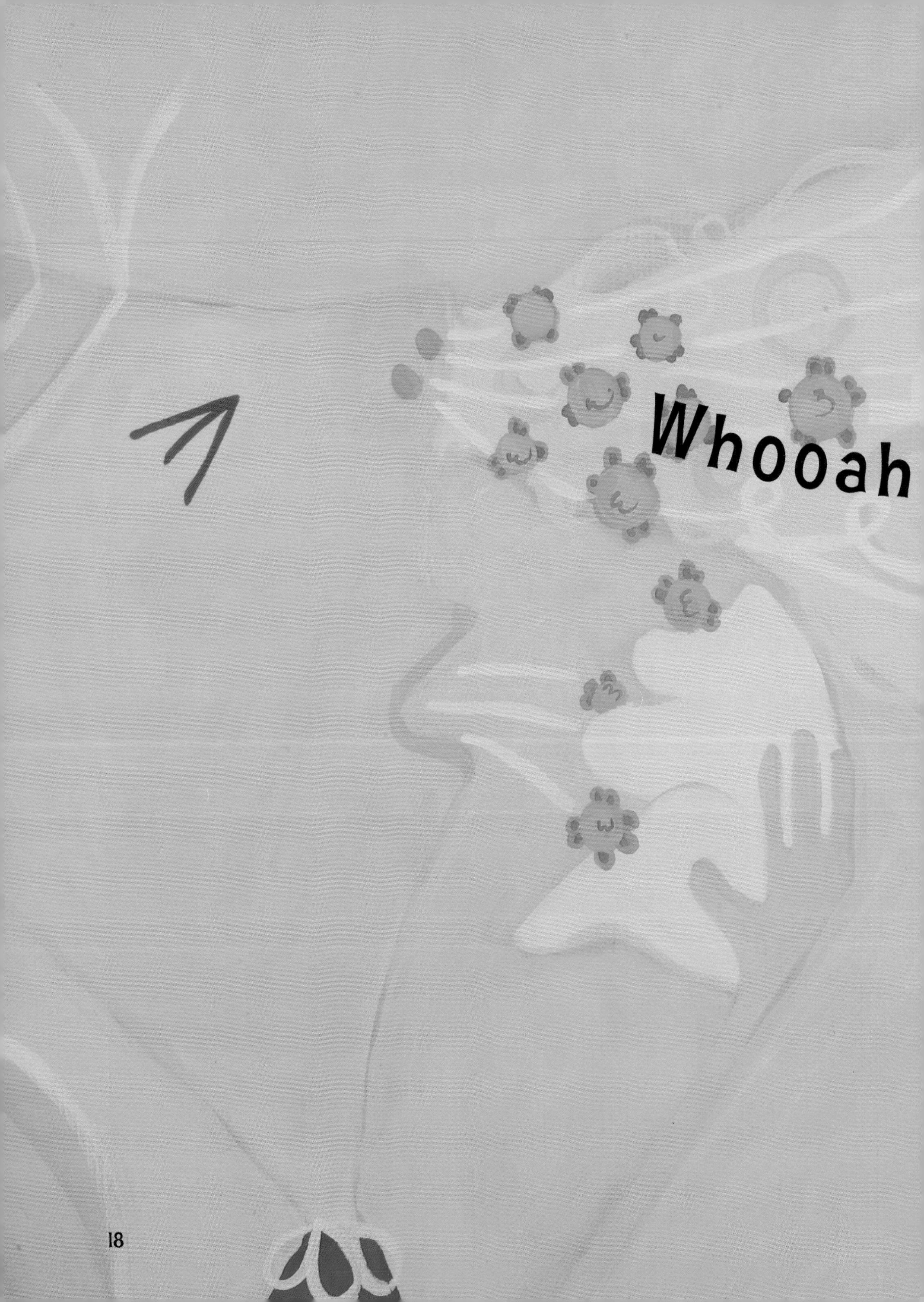
Whooah

Rhin-Rhin O'Virus
was very,
very pleased.

She had waited patiently on a cold, shiny planet and finally she had been picked up and put in just the place she had hoped. She wasted no time. She rushed through the forests until she found a nice big building, and she used her secret key.

"I'm going to have the
biggest party of all,"

she giggled.

Rhiniwun

Rhin-Rhin wriggled
out of her
space suit.

Rhin-Rhin

Rhinitoo

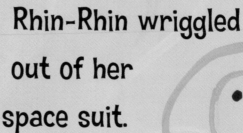

**She hopped and
skipped and slid around.**
She knocked things **over**
and **pulled things down.**

And she found some copying
machines and set about making
herself playmates—just like
herself. Rhiniwun and Rhinitoo,
Rhinithri and Rhinifor, Rhinifive
and Rhinisix,

Rhinifive

Rhiniseven

Rhinisix

Rhiniseven
and Rhinimore . . .

Soon, there were almost
six hundred thousand, two
hundred and thirty-two of them.
The building was bursting. There was
hardly room for them all!

They wiggled and wriggled.
They jiggled and pranced.
They whirled and twirled.

They played Duck
Duck Goose.
**They played
Simon Says.**

And they made
a big, big mess.

GOOSE!

And when there
was no more
room . . .

600232nd

. . . they broke into
other buildings and
made even more
like themselves.
And soon, there were one
million, one hundred thousand, three
hundred and twenty-two
of them!
What a party!
And what a huge,
HUGE MESS!

But not for long . . .

26

The police soon found them and the party was over. And soon they felt it come . . . that **whoosh, whistle, rumble!**

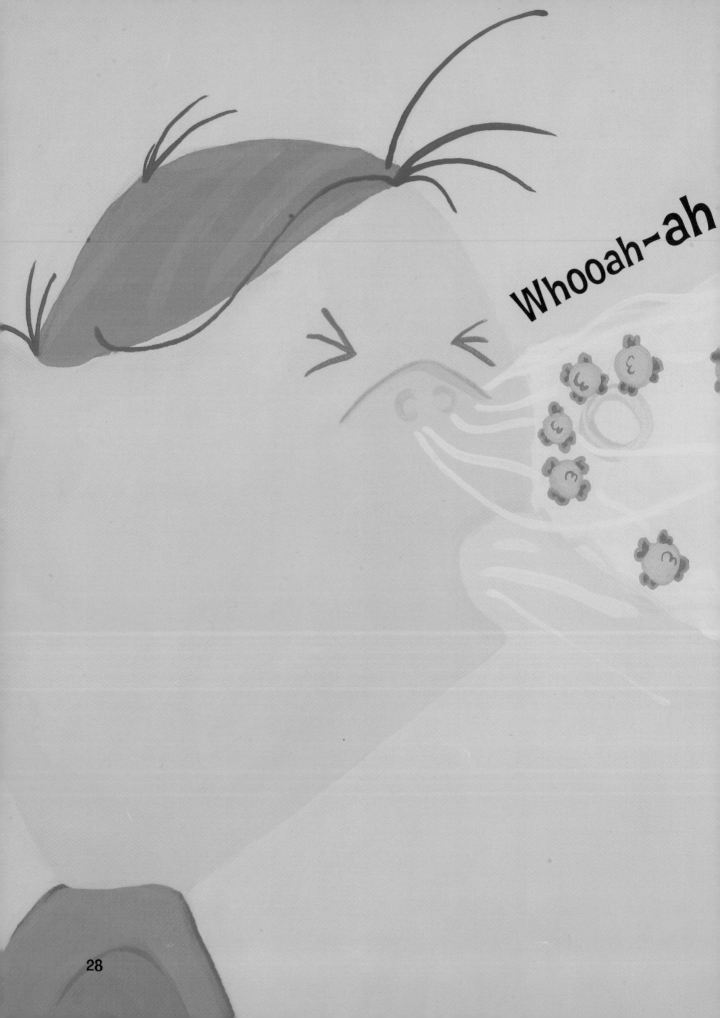

The Biology of a Cold

Colds are caused by viruses, which are pieces of genetic material in a protective encasing. The most common cold virus, the Rhinovirus, gets its name from the Greek word Rhin, which means 'nose'. Cold viruses come in through our nose or mouth and enter the cells in the top of the nose or respiratory pathway. This is done using a special key on their protective covering that binds to a 'receptor' or door on the surface of the cell , causing it to open up and let them in. Inside they use the machinery of the cell to make copies of themselves, including the genetic material and the elements of their protective covering . This is the same machinery that the cell uses to copy and readout the instructions of its own DNA, a process that goes on all the time in every cell, keeping our body working the way it should.

Virus infected cells send out a signal that activates the immune system of our body. Our immune system fights these virus invaders with antibodies that stick to the viruses and prevent them from doing further damage, T-cells that can recognize and destroy infected cells, and macrophages that clean up the debris.

Usually we don't even know we have a cold until the immune response is activated, which often takes at least a day. The best way to prevent a cold is to wash your hands frequently, especially if you have been in the way of somebody's cough or sneeze!

To learn more
about viruses and the
inside of the cell,
visit our website at
www.magicworldmedia.com/
JigJiggleSneeze

For my wonderful kids, whose noses are always
running, wash your hands! –J.V.

To David, Jack, Georgia Mae and Rhoda,
my inspirational family. -J.D.

For more information on text and illustrations visit www.magicworldmedia.com

Copyright © 2009 Magic World Media LLC

All rights reserved, including the right of reproduction in whole or in part in any form.

ISBN-13: 978-0-9821141-2-4 / ISBN-10: 0-9821141-2-5

Library of Congress Card Number: 2008940171

Printed in India